Bed Among the Lent...

A monologue from *Talking Heads*

Alan Bennett

Samuel French—London

FOR AMATEUR PRODUCTION ENQUIRIES

UNITED KINGDOM AND WORLD EXCLUDING NORTH AMERICA

plays@SamuelFrench-London.co.uk

020 7255 4302/01

Each title is subject to availability from Samuel French, depending upon country of performance.

BED AMONG THE LENTILS

First shown on BBC TV on May 3rd, 1988. The cast was as follows:

Susan   Maggie Smith

Directed by Alan Bennett
Produced by Innes Lloyd
Designed by Tony Burrough

Subsequently performed as part of the stage version of *Talking Heads*, which opened on 7th June, 1996, at the Minerva Theatre, Chichester, transferring to the Comedy Theatre, London. The cast was as follows:

Susan   Maggie Smith

Directed by Alan Bennett
Designed by Simon Higlett

AUTHOR'S NOTE

The set should be kept simple. There is no point in constructing an elaborate set (still less a series of sets) and just putting one person in the middle of it all. Less, in this case, is more; the simpler the setting, the more the audience is required to use its imagination and concentrate on the performer. If you want costumes and scenery do *Carousel.*

Other plays by Alan Bennett published by
Samuel French Ltd:

Enjoy

Getting On

Habeas Corpus

Kafka's Dick (revised)

Office Suite
Green Forms *and* A Visit from Miss Prothero

The Old Country

Say Something Happened

Single Spies
An Englishman Abroad *and* A Question of Attribution

Talking Heads:
A Chip in the Sugar
A Cream Cracker Under the Settee
Her Big Chance
A Lady of Letters
Soldiering On
A Woman of No Importance

BED AMONG THE LENTILS

The kitchen. Morning

There is an upright chair, another chair and a dresser, but no elaborate furnishings

Music. The Lights come up

Susan sits in the upright chair. She is a vicar's wife and is dressed accordingly. She is thin and nervous. (N.B. She is not drunk at any point in the play)

The music fades

Susan Geoffrey's bad enough but I'm glad I wasn't married to Jesus. The lesson this morning was the business in the Garden of Gethsemane when Jesus prays and the disciples keep falling asleep. He wakes them up and says, 'Could you not watch with me one hour?' It's my mother.

I overslept this morning, flung on a cardigan and got there just as everybody was standing up. It was Holy Communion so the militants were out in force, the sub-zero temperature in the side-chapel doubtless adding to the attraction.

Geoffrey kicks off by apologising for his failure to de-frost the church. (Subdued merriment.) Mr Medlicott has shingles, Geoffrey explains, and, as is well known, has consistently refused to initiate us lesser mortals into the mysteries of the boiler. (Helpless laughter.)

Mrs Belcher read the lesson. Mr Belcher took the plate round. 'Big
day for you,' I said to them afterwards.

The sermon was about sex. I didn't actually nod off, though I have
heard it before. Marriage gives the OK to sex is the gist of it, but
while it is far from being the be all and end all (you can say that again)
sex is nevertheless the supreme joy of the married state and a symbol
of the relationship between us and God. So, Geoffrey concludes,
when we put our money in the plate it is a symbol of everything in
our lives we are offering to God and that includes our sex. I could
only find 10p.

Thinking about the sermon during the hymn I felt a pang of
sympathy for the Deity, gifted with all this sex. No fun being made
a present of the rare and desiccated conjunctions that take place
between Geoffrey and me. Or the frightful collisions that presumably
still occur between the Belchers. Not to mention whatever
shamefaced fumblings go on between Miss Budd and Miss Bantock.
'It's all right if we offer it to God, Alice.' 'Well. if you say so,
Pauline.'

Amazing scenes at the church door. Geoffrey had announced that
after Easter the bishop would be paying us a visit so the fan club were
running round in small circles, Miss Frobisher even going so far as
to squeeze my elbow. Meanwhile, Geoffrey stands there, the wind
billowing out his surplice and ruffling his hair, what 'Who's Who
in the Diocese of Ripon' calls 'his schoolboy good looks'. I helped
put away the books while he did his 'underneath this cassock I an
but a man like anybody else' act. 'Such a live wire,' said Mr
Belcher, 'really putting the parish on the map.' 'That's right,
burbles Mrs Shrubsole, looking at me. 'We must cherish him.'

We came back and I cherished him with some chicken wings in ;
tuna fish sauce. He said, 'That went down well.' I said, 'The chicker
wings?' He said, 'My sermon. I felt it hit the nail on the head.' He
put his hand over mine, hoping, I suppose, that having hit one nail
he might hit another, but I said I had to go round with the parish
magazine. 'Good girl,' he said. 'I can attack my paperwork instead.'

Roads busy. Sunday afternoon. Families having a run out. Wheeling the pram, walking the dog. Living. Almighty God unto whom all hearts be open, and from whom no secrets are hid, cleanse the thoughts of our hearts by the inspiration of thy Holy Spirit that we may perfectly love thee and worthily magnify thy glorious name and not spend our Sunday afternoons parked in a lay-by on the Ring Road wondering what happened to our life.

When I got back Geoffrey was just off to Evensong, was I going to come? When I said 'No' he said, 'Really? Then I'd better pretend you have a headache.'

Why? One of the unsolved mysteries of life, or the unsolved mysteries of my life, is why the vicar's wife is expected to go to church at all. A barrister's wife doesn't have to go to court, an actor's wife isn't at every performance, so why have I always got to be on parade? Not to mention the larger question of whether one believes in God in the first place. It's assumed that being the vicar's wife one does but the question has never actually come up, not with Geoffrey anyway. I can understand why, of course. To look at me, the hair, the flat chest, the wan smile, you'd think I was just cut out for God. And maybe I am. I'd just like to have been asked that's all. Not that it matters of course. So long as you can run a tight jumble sale you can believe in what you like.

It could be that Geoffrey doesn't believe in God either. I've always longed to ask him only God never seems to crop up. 'Geoffrey,' I'd say. 'Yes, Susan?' 'Do you really believe in God? I mean, cards on tables, you don't honestly, do you? God's just a job like any other. You've got to bring home the bacon somehow.' But no. Not a word. The subject's never discussed.

After he'd gone I discovered we were out of sherry so I've just been round to the off-licence. The woman served me. Didn't smile. I can't think why. I spend enough.

Music. The Lights fade

Susan exits. She puts on a coat or pinny and collects an altar candlestick and cloth. She re-enters and starts to polish the candlestick

The Lights come up on the same setting. The music fades. Afternoon

We were discussing the ordination of women. The bishop asked me what I thought. Should women take the services? So long as it doesn't have to be me, I wanted to say, they can be taken by a trained gorilla. 'Oh yes,' Geoffrey chips in, 'Susan's all in favour. She's keener than I am, aren't you, darling?' 'More sprouts anybody?' I said.

On the young side for a bishop, but he's been a prominent sportsman at university so that would explain it. Boxing or rugby. Broken nose at some stage anyway. One of the 'Christianity is common sense' brigade. Hobby's bricklaying apparently and refers to me throughout as 'Mrs Vicar'. Wants beer with his lunch and Geoffrey says he'll join him so this leaves me with the wine. Geoffrey's all over him because the rumour is he's shopping round for a new Archdeacon. Asks Geoff how outgoing I am. Actually says that. 'How outgoing is Mrs Vicar?' Mr Vicar jumps in with a quick rundown of my accomplishments and an outline of my punishing schedule. On a typical day, apparently, I kick off by changing the wheel on the Fiesta, then hasten to the bedside of a dying pensioner, after which, having done the altar flowers and dispensed warmth and appreciation to sundry parishioners en route, I top off a thrill-packed morning by taking round Meals on Wheels . . . somehow — 'and this to me is the miracle,' says Geoffrey — 'somehow managing to rustle up a delicious lunch in the interim', the miracle somewhat belied by the flabby lasagne we are currently embarked on. 'The ladies,' says the bishop. 'Where would we be without them?'

Disaster strikes as I'm doling out the tinned peaches: the jug into which I've decanted the Carnation milk gets knocked over, possibly by me. Geoffrey, for whom turning the other cheek is part of the job, claims it caught his elbow and his lordship takes the same line, insisting he gets doused in Carnation milk practically every day of his life. Still, when I get a dishcloth and sponge off his gaiters I catch him giving me a funny look. It's Mary Magdalen and the Nivea cream all over again. After lunch Geoffrey's supposed to be taking him on a tour of the parish but while we're having a cup of instant he claps his hand to his temple because he's suddenly remembered he's supposed to be in Keighley blessing a steam engine.

We're stacking the dishwasher and I ask Geoffrey how he thinks it's gone. Doesn't know. 'Fingers crossed,' I say. 'I think there are more constructive things we could do than that,' he says crisply, and goes off to mend his inner tube. I sit by the Aga for a bit and as I doze off it comes to me that by 'constructive things' he perhaps means prayer.

When I wake up there's a note from Geoffrey. 'Gone to talk to the Ladies Bright Hour. Go to bed.' I'm not sleepy and anyway we're running low on sherry so I drive into Leeds. I've stopped going round the corner now as I owe them a bit on the side and she's always so surly. There's a little Indian shop behind the Infirmary I've found. It's a newsagents basically but it sells drink and anything really, the way they do. Open last thing at night, Sundays included, my ideal. Ramesh he's called. Mr Ramesh I call him, though Ramesh may be his Christian name. Only not Christian of course. I've been once or twice now, only this time he sits me in the back place on a sack of something and talks. Little statuette of a god on the wall. A god. Not The God. Not the definite article. One of several thousand apparently. 'Safety in numbers,' I said but he didn't understand. Looks a bit more fun than Jesus anyway. Shows me pictures of other gods, getting up to all sorts. I said, 'She looks a very busy lady. Is that yoga?' He said, 'Well, it helps.' He's quite athletic himself apparently, married, but his wife's only about fourteen so they won't let her in. He calls me Mrs Vicar too, only it's different. He has lovely teeth.

Music. The Lights fade

The Lights come up on the same setting. Morning

Once upon a time I had my life planned out — or half of it at any rate. I wasn't clear about the first part, but at the stroke of fifty I was all set to turn into a wonderful woman — the wife to a doctor, or a vicar's wife, Chairman of the Parish Council, a pillar of the WI. A wise, witty and ultimately white-haired old lady, who's always stood on her own feet until one day at the age of eighty she comes out of the County Library, falls under the weight of her improving book, breaks her hip and dies peacefully, continently and without fuss under a snowy coverlet in the cottage hospital. And coming away from her funeral in a country churchyard on a bright winter's afternoon people would say, 'Well, she was a wonderful woman.'

Had this been a serious ambition I should have seen to it I was equipped with the skills necessary to its achievement. How to produce jam which, after reaching a good, rolling boil, successfully coats the spoon; how to whip up a Victoria sponge that just gives to the fingertips; how to plan, execute and carry through a successful garden fête. All weapons in the armoury of any upstanding Anglican lady. But I can do none of these things. I'm even a fool at the flower arrangement. I ought to have a PhD in the subject the number of classes I've been to but still my efforts show as much evidence of art as walking sticks in an umbrella stand. Actually it's temperament. I don't have it. If you think squash is a competitive activity try flower arrangement.

On this particular morning the rota has Miss Frobisher and Mrs Belcher down for the side aisles and I'm paired with Mrs Shrubsole to do the altar and the lectern. My honest opinion, never voiced needless to say, is that if they were really sincere about religion they'd forget flower arrangement altogether, invest in some permanent plastic jobs and put the money towards the current most popular famine. However, around mid-morning I wander over to the church with a few dog-eared chrysanthemums. They look as if they could do with an immediate drink so I call in at the vestry and root out a vase or two from the cupboard where Geoffrey keeps the communion wine.

It not looming very large on my horizon, I assume I am doing the altar and Mrs Shrubsole the lectern, but when I come out of the vestry Mrs S is at the altar well embarked on her arrangement. I said, 'I thought I was doing the altar.' She said, 'No. I think Mrs Belcher will bear me out. I'm down to do the altar. You are doing the lectern. Why?' She smiled sweetly. 'Do you have a preference?' The only preference I have is to shove my chrysanthemums up her nose but instead I practise a bit of Christian forbearance and go stick them in a vase by the lectern. In the best tradition of my floral arrangements they look like the poles of a wigwam, so I go and see if I can cadge a bit of backing from Mrs Belcher. 'Are you using this?' I say, picking up a bit of mouldy old fern. 'I certainly am. I need every bit of my spiraea. It gives it body.' I go over and see if Miss Frobisher has any greenery going begging only she's doing some Japanese number, a vase like a test-tube half-filled with gravel, in which she's throttling a lone carnation. So I retire to the vestry for a bit to calm my shattered nerves, and when I come out ready to tackle my chrysanths again Mrs Shrubsole has apparently finished and fetched the other two up to the altar to admire her handiwork. So I wander up and take a look.

Well, it's a brown job, beech leaves, teasels, grass, that school of thought. Mrs Shrubsole is saying, 'It's called Forest Murmurs. It's what I did for my Highly Commended at Harrogate last year. What do you think?' Gert and Daisy are of course speechless with admiration, but when I tentatively suggest it might look a bit better if she cleared up all the bits and pieces lying around she said, 'What bits and pieces?' I said, 'All these acorns and fir-cones and what not. What's this conker in aid of?' She said, 'Leave that. The whole arrangement pivots on that.' I said, 'Pivots?' 'When the adjudicator was commenting on my arrangement he particularly singled out the hint I gave of the forest floor.' I said, 'Mrs Shrubsole. This is the altar of St Michael and All Angels. It is not *The Wind in the Willows*.' Mrs Belcher said, 'I think you ought to sit down.' I said, 'I do not want to sit down.' I said, 'It's all very well to transform the altar into something out of Bambi but do not forget that for the vicar the altar is his working surface. Furthermore,' I added, 'should the vicar sink to his knees in prayer, which since this is the altar he is wont to do, he is quite likely to get one of these teasel things in his eye. This is not a flower arrangement. It is a booby trap. Permit me to demonstrate.' And I begin getting down on my knees just to prove how lethal her bloody Forest Murmurs is. Only I must have slipped because next thing I know I'm rolling down the altar steps and end up banging my head on the communion rail.

Mrs Shrubsole, who along with every other organization known to man has been in the St John's Ambulance Brigade, wants me left lying down, whereas Mrs Belcher is all for getting me on to a chair. 'Leave them lying down,' says Mrs Belcher, 'and they inhale their own vomit. It happens all the time, Veronica.' 'Only, Muriel,' says Mrs Shrubsole, 'when they have vomited. She hasn't vomited. 'No,' I say, 'but I will if I have to listen to any more of this drivel,' and begin to get up. 'Is that blood, Veronica?' says Mrs Belcher pointing to my head. 'Well,' says Mrs Shrubsole, reluctant to concede to Mrs B on any matter remotely touching medicine, 'it could be, I suppose. What we need is some hot sweet tea.' 'I thought that theory had been discredited,' says Mrs Belcher. Discredited or not it sends Miss Frobisher streaking off to find a teabag and also, it subsequently transpires, to telephone all and sundry in an effort to locate Geoffrey. He is in York taking part in the usual interdenominational conference on the role of the church in a hitherto uncolonised department of life, underfloor central heating possibly. He comes haring back thinking I'm at death's door, and finding I'm not has nothing more constructive to offer than I take a nap.

This gives the fan club the green light to invade the vicarage, making endless tea and the vicar his lunch and, as he puts it, 'spoiling him rotten'. Since this also licenses them to conduct a fact-finding survey of all the housekeeping arrangements or absence of same ('Where does she keep the Duraglit, vicar?'), a good time is had by all. Meanwhile Emily Brontë is laid out on the sofa in a light doze.

I come round to hear Geoffrey saying, 'Mrs Shrubsole's going now, darling.' I don't get up. I never even open my eyes. I just wave and say, 'Goodbye, Mrs Shrubsole.' Only thinking about it as I drift off again I think I may have said, 'Goodbye, Mrs Subsoil.'

When I woke up it was dark and Geoffrey'd gone out. I couldn't find
a thing in the cupboard so I got the car out and drove into Leeds. I
sat in the shop for a bit, not saying much. Then I felt a bit wanny and
Mr Ramesh let me go into the back place to lie down. I must have
dozed off because when I woke up Mr Ramesh has come in and
started taking off his clothes. I said, 'What are you doing? What
about the shop?' He said, 'Do not worry about the shop. I have
closed the shop.' I said, 'It's only nine. You don't close till eleven.'
'I do tonight,' he said. I said, 'What's tonight?' He said, 'A chance
in a million. A turn-up for the books. Will you take your clothes off
please.' And I did.

Music. The Lights fade

Susan exits

The Lights come up and the music fades. Afternoon

*Susan enters wearing a shabby raincoat and carrying an old
shopping bag. She puts the bag down carefully so that the bottles
inside do not clink*

You never see pictures of Jesus smiling, do you? I mentioned this
to Geoffrey once. 'Good point, Susan,' is what he said, which made
me wish I'd not brought it up in the first place. Said I should think
of Our Lord as having an inward smile, the doctrine according to
Geoffrey being that Jesus was made man so he smiled, laughed and
did everything else just like the rest of us. 'Do you think he ever
smirked?' I asked, whereupon Geoffrey suddenly remembered he
was burying somebody in five minutes and took himself off.

If Jesus is all man I just wish they'd put a bit more of it into the
illustrations. I was sitting in church yesterday, wrestling with this
point of theology, when it occurred to me that something seemed to
have happened to Geoffrey. The service should have kicked off ages
ago but he's still in the vestry. Mr Bland is filling in with something
uplifting on the organ and Miss Frobisher, never one to let an
opportunity slip, has slumped to her knees for a spot of unscheduled

silent prayer. Mrs Shrubsole is lost in contemplation of the altar, still adorned with Forest Murmurs, a trail of ivy round the cross the final inspired touch. Mr Bland now ups the volume but still no sign of Geoff. 'Arnold,' says Mrs Belcher, 'there seems to be some hiatus in the proceedings,' and suddenly the fan club is on red alert. She's just levering him to his feet when I get in first and nip in there to investigate.

His reverence is there, white-faced, every cupboard open and practically in tears. He said, 'Have you seen it?' I said, 'What?' He said, 'The wine. The communion wine. It's gone.' I said, 'That's no tragedy,' and offer to pop out and get some ordinary. Geoffrey said, 'They're not open. Besides, what does it look like?' I said, 'Well, it looks like we've run out of communion wine.' He said, 'We haven't run out. There was a full bottle here on Friday. Somebody has drunk it.'

It's on the tip of my tongue to say that if Jesus is all he's cracked up to be why doesn't he use tap-water and put it to the test when I suddenly remember that Mr Bland keeps a bottle of cough mixture in his cupboard in case any of the choirboys gets chesty. At the thought of celebrating the Lord's Supper in Benylin Geoffrey now has a complete nervous breakdown but, as I point out, it's red and sweet and nobody is going to notice. Nor do they. I see Mr Belcher licking his lips a bit thoughtfully as he walks back down the aisle but that's all. 'What was the delay?' asks Mrs Shrubsole. 'Nothing,' I said, 'just a little hiccup.'

Having got it right for once I'm feeling quite pleased with myself but Geoffrey obviously isn't and never speaks all afternoon so I bunk off Evensong and go into Leeds.

Mr Ramesh has evidently been expecting me because there's a bed made up in the storeroom upstairs. I go up first and get in. When I'm in bed I can put my hand out and feel the lentils running through my fingers. When he comes up he's put on his proper clothes. Long white shirt, sash and what not. Loincloth underneath. All spotless.

Like Jesus. Only not. I watch him undress and think about them all at Evensong and Geoffrey praying in that pausy way he does, giving you time to mean each phrase. And the fan club lapping it up, thinking they love God when they just love Geoffrey. Lighten our darkness we beseech thee O Lord and by thy great mercy defend us from all perils and dangers of this night. Like Mr Ramesh who is twenty-six with lovely legs, who goes swimming every morning at Merrion Street Baths and plays hockey for Horsforth. I ask him if they offer their sex to God. He isn't very interested in the point but with them, so far as I can gather, sex is all part of God anyway. I can see why too. It's the first time I really understand what all the fuss is about. There among the lentils on the second Sunday after Trinity.

I've just popped into the vestry. He's put a lock on the cupboard door.

She picks up the bag and heads for the exit. The bag clinks slightly so that we know it contains bottles

Music. The Lights fade

Susan exits, changes quickly and re-enters

The Lights come up. The music fades. Evening. Susan is wearing a neat costume, with her hair done. She seems a different woman

I stand up and say, 'My name is Susan. I am a vicar's wife and I am an alcoholic.' Then I tell my story. Or some of it anyway. 'Don't pull any punches,' says Clem, my counsellor. 'Nobody's going to be shocked, believe me love, we've all been there.' But I don't tell them about Mr Ramesh because they've not been there. 'Listen, people. I was so drunk I used to go and sleep with an Asian grocer. Yes, and you won't believe this. I loved it. Loved every minute.' Dear oh dear. This was a real drunken lady.

So I draw a veil over Mr Ramesh who once, on the feast of St Simon and St Jude (Choral Evensong at six, daily services at the customary

hour), put make-up on his eyes and bells on his ankles, and naked
except for his little belt danced in the back room of the shop with a
tambourine.

'So how did you come to AA?' they ask. 'My husband,' I say. 'The
vicar. He persuaded me.' But I lie. It was not my husband, it was Mr
Ramesh, the exquisitely delicate and polite Mr Ramesh who one
Sunday night turned his troubled face towards me with its struggling
moustache and asked if he might take the bull by the horns and
enquire if intoxication was a prerequisite for sexual intercourse, or
whether it was only when I was going to bed with him, the beautiful
Mr Ramesh, twenty-six, with wonderful legs, whether it was only
with him I had to be inebriated. And was it, asked this slim, flawless
and troubled creature, was it perhaps his colour? Because if not he
would like to float the suggestion that sober might be even nicer. So
the credit for the road to Damascus goes to Mr Ramesh, whose first
name turns out also to be Ramesh. Ramesh Ramesh, a member of
the community council and the Leeds Federation of Trade.

But none of this I say. In fact I never say anything at all. Only when
it becomes plain to Geoffrey (and it takes all of three weeks) that Mrs
Vicar is finally on the wagon, who is it gets the credit? Not one of
Mr Ramesh's jolly little gods, busy doing everything under the sun
to one another, much like Mr Ramesh. Oh no. It's full marks to
Geoffrey's chum, the Deity, moving in his well-known mysterious
way.

So now everything has changed. For the moment I am a new woman
and Geoffrey is a new man. And he brings it up on the slightest
pretext. 'My wife's an alcoholic, you know. Yes. It's a great
challenge to me and to the parish as extended family.' From being
a fly in the ointment I find myself transformed into a feather in his
cap. Included it in his sermon on Prayers Answered when he reveals
that he and the fan club have been having these jolly get-togethers
in which they'd all prayed over what he calls 'my problem'. It
practically sent me racing back to the Tio Pepe even to think of it.
The fans, of course, never dreaming that their prayers would be

answered, are furious. They think it's brought us closer together. Geoffrey thinks that too. We were at some doleful diocesan jamboree last week and I'm stuck there clutching my grapefruit juice as Geoffrey's telling the tale to some bearded cleric. Suddenly he seizes my hand. 'We met it with love,' he cries, as if love were some all-purpose antibiotic, which to Geoffrey it probably is.

And it goes on, the mileage in it endless. I said to Geoffrey that when I stood up at AA I sometimes told the story about the flower arranging. Result: he starts telling it all over the diocese. The first time was at a conference on The Supportive Parish. Gales of deep, liberated, caring laughter. He's now given it a new twist and tells the story as if he's talking about a parishioner, then at the end he says, 'Friends I want to tell you something. (Deep hush.) That drunken flower-arranger was my wife.' Silence ... then the applause, *terrific*.

I've caught the other young, upwardly mobile parsons sneaking looks at me now and again and you can see them thinking why weren't they smart enough to marry an alcoholic or better still a drug addict, problem wives whom they could do a nice redemption job on, right there on their own doorstep. Because there's no stopping Geoffrey now. He grips my hand in public, nay brandishes it. 'We're a team,' he cries. Looks certain to be rural dean and that's only the beginning. As the bishop says, 'Just the kind of man we're looking for on the bench — someone with a seasoned compassion, someone who's looked life in the face. Someone who's been there.'

Mr Ramesh sold his shop. He's gone back to India to fetch his wife. She's old enough now apparently. I went down there on Sunday. There was a boy writing Under New Management on the window. Spelled wrong. And something underneath in Hindi, spelled right probably. He said he thought Mr Ramesh would be getting another shop, only in Preston.

They do that, of course, Asians, build something up, get it going nicely, then take the profit and move on. It's a good thing. We ought to be more like that, more enterprising.

My group meets twice a week and I go. Religiously. And that's what it is, of course. The names are different, Frankie and Steve, Susie and Clem. But it's actually Miss Frobisher and Mrs Shrubsole all over again. I never liked going to one church so I end up going to two. Geoffrey would call that the wonderful mystery of God. I call it bad taste. And I wouldn't do it to a dog. But that's the thing nobody ever says about God — he has no taste at all.

Music. The Lights fade to Black-out

FURNITURE AND PROPERTY LIST

On stage: Upright chair
Chair
Dresser

Off stage: Altar candlestick
Polishing cloth
Shopping bag containing bottles

LIGHTING PLOT

Practical fittings required: nil
Interior. The same scene throughout

To open: General interior lighting; morning setting

Cue 1	**Susan**: "I spend enough." Music *Fade lights*	(Page 3)
Cue 2	**Susan** start to polish the candlestick *Bring up lights; afternoon setting*	(Page 4)
Cue 3	**Susan**: "He has lovely teeth." Music *Fade lights*	(Page 5)
Cue 4	When ready *Bring up lights; morning setting*	(Page 5)
Cue 5	**Susan**: "And I did." Music *Fade lights*	(Page 9)
Cue 6	**Susan** exits; then, when ready *Bring up lights; afternoon setting*	(Page 9)
Cue 7	**Susan** heads for the exit. Music *Fade lights*	(Page 11)
Cue 8	**Susan** re-enters *Bring up lights; evening setting*	(Page 11)
Cue 9	**Susan**: " — he has no taste at all." Music *Fade to black-out*	(Page 14)

EFFECTS PLOT

Lightning Source UK Ltd.
Milton Keynes UK
UKOW06f0815060716

277735UK00001B/272/P

9 780573 132247